THE WORLD IN YOUR HANDS

BEGINNERS GUIDE TO PALMISTRY COUNSELLING

JOHN HARRISON

authorHOUSE®

AuthorHouse™ UK
1663 Liberty Drive
Bloomington, IN 47403 USA
www.authorhouse.co.uk
Phone: 0800 047 8203 (Domestic TFN)
*   +44 1908 723714 (International)*

Published by AuthorHouse 06/24/2019

ISBN: 978-1-7283-8940-0 (sc)
ISBN: 978-1-7283-8941-7 (e)

CONTENTS

FIGURES

INTRODUCTION TO PALMISTRY COUNSELLING?

Palmistry Counselling is a wonderful form of guidance and advice because it covers all areas of your life in great detail and offers an interpretation of your life purpose! So, whether you are interested in your health, career, relationship, or the more in-depth issues of psychology, philosophy or spirituality, palmistry counselling provides the answers. Of particular importance is the fact that a Reading covers the every area of your life, rather than just the next few years.

This is an ancient discipline, which originates from the Sacred Sanskrit Texts of the Indian Sub-Continent called The Vedas; it is thought to have been conceived thousands of years before now. Strongly associated with Astrology, Aristotle brought it to the West, and great men and women throughout history such as Napolean Bonaparte consulted Chiromancy [Hand Magic].

WHAT CAN PALMISTRY COUNSELLING DO FOR YOU?

In short, it can provide you with the ANSWERS that can help you solve your problems! Palmistry counselling is a modern profession created by John Harrison. It draws upon Astrological Symbolism, such as the meanings of the Planets and Stars [known to you through your Birth Chart], and the Elements, Earth, Air, Fire, and Water. Every good Palmistry Counsellor should be knowledgeable concerning the Science of Chirology [Hand Analysis], which is the basis for interpreting the hands. But palmistry counselling is so much more than just the ability to assess character, personality, profession or romantic orientation, it is also meant for when we apply intuition, psychic insight, and a working knowledge of psychology, then the counselling and empowerment for you to change your life for the better comes into its own element. The result is to give you a deep, meaningful, and comprehensive framework for living your life productively, thereby transforming your attitudes to work, maintenance of your health in harmony with nature, and how to be happier in all your relationships. The reason for this, in a nutshell, is rather than just receiving a one-off interpretation of what's happening now, or what are the future trends, you are given the tools to influence your own destiny, and the power to transform your whole approach to life, and make it more likely to attain health, wealth, and happiness.

SO, WHAT ARE YOUR QUESTIONS?

Do you need to know what you need to do to improve your health?Or, perhaps help you to recover from a complaint?Are you aware that prominent physicians, such as Dr Charlotte Wolfe, and Doctor Benham used to diagnose illnesses by feeling the hands before now?

HOW CAN YOU IMPROVE YOUR HEALTH ?

Are you in need of advice about your health?What do your Hands tell you about your present lifestyle?Do you need to address your addictions, ie drinking, smoking, etcHow long will you live?What can you do to live a vibrant, healthy life?

Relationships in love can also be discerned.

ARE YOU COMPATIBLE WITH YOUR PARTNER?

Are your characters and personalities complimentary or antagonistic?Do you see yourself getting married, having children, finding love and happiness?And how will you relate to your children?Will you stay together, separate, or will you get back together with a lost lover?

WHAT CAREER PATH SHOULD YOU CHOOSE?

Are you out of work, and seeking a new career direction?Have you moved residence to a different location, and wondering if you will find a suitable job?Perhaps your career is in the doldrums, and are you seeking a fresh start?Would it be best for you to be self -employed, gain more qualifications or chose a new profession?Are you better suited to a vocation, such as teaching, nursing or working for a charity?Finally, maybe you have decided to give up work to nurture children or go travelling

Palmistry holds the answers to these questions, and also the larger picture, such as the actual purpose of your life; what you are here for, and what you can do to transform your life!!!

HOW CAN PALMISTRY COUNSELLING TELL YOU ALL THIS?

According to Astrology, the positions of the Planets and Stars affect our lives. And the Elements in a Chart are significant to your personal life. Does this all sound a bit irrational, or superstitious?Well, No, not really!!!We all know that the Moon affects our moods, women's menstrual cycles, and the weather!The Sun similarly regulates our climate, from growing crops to drought. So, it is quite plausible that the Planets such as Jupiter, Saturn as well as the more distant Stars have a subtle, but vital role to play in our lives. The reason for this at a deep level is that everything in the Universe is connected by a stream of energy, like waves or currents that ebb and flow, that create harmony or conflict. When we "go with the flow", all goes well in our life; but when we swim against the tide, troubles arise. So sometimes it is best to "sit tight" and wait, while at other times, we should surge forward optimistically. The trick is to find out when the most auspicious times for growth are, but also when we should hold back and wait. Fortunately, palmistry counselling enables us to learn these important lessons in safety and security, so that we become wiser and be in control of our lives.

WHY PALMISTRY COUNSELLING WORKS.......LIKE MAGIC?

There are 3 Categories within **Palmistry**.

Chirognomy -The Shape of the Hands[your character and personality]. Chiromancy- The Features of the Palms, i.e. Lines [your Map of Life; or direction]. Dermatoglyphics-The Finger Prints and Skin Ridge Patterns [your mental and social conditioning; or cultural setting].

CHIROGNOMY - THE HAND SHAPES

From the 4 Different Hand Shapes, we can determine;*Your Health, Stamina, Energy, and potential longevity*Your Psychology, Philosophy, interest in Religion or Politics.*Through Hand Shape Synastry, how you will relate to Partners or your children, i.e. compatibility.*The best range of careers suited to you, and why this is so!

CHIROMANCY-THE MAP OF YOUR LIFE.

Looking at your hands, you may notice that there are probably lots of lines and bumps, and the texture of the skin may be rough or smooth? Well to the experienced palmistry counsellor this is like a Map that can be read, determining what direction you may choose to take in life, i.e. your Journey in life. But also, what route NOT to take, and why! So, it's easy, isn't it? Take the right road and end up at your destination OR take the wrong highway, and end up lost, or in trouble, i.e. a roadblock or cliff?

EXAMPLES OF WHY THIS IS TRUE!

The Life Line indicates your general physical health, and life force energy, or endurance. The Heart Line shows your emotional response to life, feelings, and romantic inclinations. The Head Line indicates your psychology, i.e. thoughtful or impetuous; logical or imaginative. The Fate Line shows your Life Purpose, your vocation and faith, and how Events unfold. The Sun Line [Apollo] indicates creativity and public service; Fame and Fortune. There are many other less prominent, but still important lines, of which the most misinterpreted by amateurs must be the Marriage and Children Lines, which provide potential for happiness. Fortunately, the palmistry counsellor can not only analyse these lines under the Little Finger but can also apply psychic insight and therapeutic skills to assist you!

DERMATOGLYPHICS- INHERITED GENETIC CONDITIONING.

The Fingerprints and Skin Ridge Patterns are the most fascinating area. From a medical perspective, they represent our parent's chromosomes, known as the genetic features.

FINGERPRINTS

Whereas the Fingers, in general, represent our Mental Landscape and Psychology, the Finger Print Patterns represent our Individuality, and finely tuned beliefs, and cultural perspectivesTherefore, for example, they can indicate;• Whether you are emotional, imaginative, flexible, and adaptable.• However, are you more fixed, individualistic, unorthodox and freedom loving?• Or perhaps practical, good at business, or making crafts?• Possibly highly strung, energetic, nervous, or obsessed?All these mental characteristics make up who you are, what you think, and how you see the World, but are they fixed, or can they be changed?

The skin ridge patterns can determine:-*Your sense of humour* Whether you are serious and committed in your beliefs*If you are a born leader* Or brave, courageous, or psychic?

IN CONCLUSION

Palmistry Counselling enables you to ask the right questions, Receive the right answers for your personal needs. Apply them constructively to your circumstances and you can find your purpose in life and be in harmony with the Heavens.

You have the entire universe in your hands; so by learning the fascinating art of palmistry and with the right counselling, you can apply this knowledge to change your life for the better!

THE KEYS TO YOUR PALMISTRY STUDIES!

Anyone who decides to take a trip (let's say a visit another country), will need good advice. There are so many things to think of, and if you're not careful, you'll find yourself at the airport without some important document; be it your jewellery, might be a hat or sun-screen cream! Like a vacation, in order to enjoy palmistry you'll need a list of items so that when that beautiful moment arrives, when someone shows you their hands, you won't be confused.

'The Keys to Palmistry Counselling ' is quite a list. But before we explore these tools, we need to remember that with palmistry we are dealing with people, which means diplomacy and compassion are required. Imagine what it would be like if you went to a book store and the sales assistant was rude and bad-tempered – would you make a purchase there? No! So, even if someone asks you to look at their hands and appears casual or was joking about it, never forget the privilege, responsibility, and duty you have been given – to tell the truth **_but_** be tactful. Never underestimate the power of the spoken word to help or to injure. Remember also that we are all human and like to hear good news, so be positive and have a concerned attitude.

Now, the first lesson to be learned in palmistry is that every part of the hand has individual characteristics that can be interpreted according to the laws of chirology. From a spiritual point of view, the hand represents consciousness, showing the journey of our souls in this lifetime. Psychologically the hand represents our dreams, desires, and motivations, both through our mental and emotional experiences. Physically the hand represents our bodies and what we do with them, e.g., swimming, jogging, dancing, fighting, making love, eating, drinking, and many more activities. So the hands help us to know more about ourselves physically, psychologically, and spiritually – who we are, where we are going, and how we are going to get there. But such a map must have signs and symbols to guide us, and they do.

ASTRO-PALMISTRY –PLANETARY SYMBOLISM

KEYWORD ASSOCIATIONS

THE SUN (APOLLO)

Brilliance, creativity, communication, art, beauty, music, pleasure, public life, fame, and adventure.

MERCURY

Mental dexterity, ideology, intellect, inquisitiveness, mathematics, communications, fertility, medicine, skeletal, and nervous systems.

VENUS

Strength, passion, sensuality, love, vitality, parental influence, physical, health, food, and drink.

MARS

Temper, anger, resistance to illness, ambition, courage, assertiveness.

LOWER MARS

Bravery, strength, stamina, risk-taking.

UPPER MARS

Heroism, fortitude, aggression, charisma.

THE MOON

Spirituality, sensitivity, intuition, psychic abilities, delusions, visions, attunement, contemplation, mental instability (lunacy).

EARTH

Home, safety, physical stamina, conservation, family, cultures, societies.

JUPITER

Pride, dignity, idealism, compassion, belief, inspiration, love, elation, confidence.

SATURN

Tradition, severity, discipline, stability, administration, property, legal matters, careers, finance success.

URANUS

Invention, business acumen, change, perception of time, metabolic health, genius, dynamic creativity or destruction.

NEPTUNE

Fantasies, spirituality, mysticism, sensitivity, dreams and visions, imagination, delusions, foolishness.

PLUTO

Secrecy, intensity, addictions, sensitivity, sexuality, transcendence, healing abilities, psychic experiences, psychology.

THE HISTORY OF HAND STUDIES

Since ancient times, our ancestors have looked up into the sky, marvelling at the beauty of the stars and planets. In recorded history, the Chaldeans, Assyrians, and Egyptians began the study of Astronomy and Astrology.

Like Astrology, in Palmistry one method of hand analysis involves planetary symbols. Under this system:

the THUMB is represented by the planet MARS:

the INDEX FINGER is ruled by JUPITER:

the SECOND or MIDDLE FINGER is said to be ruled by SATURN:

the THIRD or RING FINGER is assigned to the SUN (or APOLLO):

and the FOURTH or LITTLE FINGER is ruled by MERCURY.

These characteristics are also said to rule regions or areas of the hands, called the Mounts, with an expanded planetary symbology taking in Venus, Neptune, and two regions governed by Mars, i.e., Upper Mars and Lower Mars, as well as Luna (Moon).

This system has evolved in Europe and was utilised by prominent men such as Aristotle and Augustus Caesar, but the Celts and the Romany Gypsies of Eastern Europe and Russia adopted them in later centuries. With this process, palmistry became divided into two distinct and separate groups of people; the gypsies who drew upon psychic powers and who were knowledgeable about herbalism and astrology; and the men of science who distanced themselves from the Gypsies whom they deemed as charlatans. This latter group, following the earlier Greek teachings, called themselves chirologists from the Greek word "Kheir"; which means 'hand' and "Ology", which is briefly described as "the logical study of ".

The origins of chirology are ancient, stemming from the Vedas, the Indian Sanskrit texts written 2000 years before Christ. Chirology evolved in India where it is still practiced in conjunction with Vedic astrology and Ayurvedic medicine. It also spread to China, where it became integrated over thousands of years into the Chinese Buddhist religion. Based on the Elements of Earth, Air, Fire, Water, and Ether as opposed to the Western planetary system, eastern chirology is profoundly complex; but in its simplest terms, it is based on the laws of Nature.

History often teaches us that the nature of conflict and Palmistry is no stranger to controversy. Many renowned chirologists will not associate themselves with Palmistry, claiming that it is a profession governed by fakes, frauds, confidence tricksters or demented people due to it being the "Art of Hand Divination" or Fortune Telling. Palmists, on the other hand, maintain that they are seers, possessing intuitive gifts and can accurately predict the future. This viewpoint is ridiculed by the chirologists who call themselves "Hand Analysts" and give guidance on health, career, and relationship matters. They interpret but do not predict.

As a Palmistry counsellor, I see the value of both chirology and Palmistry, i.e., analysis and intuition combined; and I teach the Western tradition of chirology, because English-speaking people, including our American, Canadian, and Australian friends who share a similar educational system, easily evaluate this.

The Map of Your Life

Palmistry is the study of hand divination, which is the map of life. Chirognomy represents the structure of your hands. Physically this is the metacarpal bones, the radial and ulnar arteries, the nerves, blood vessels and finally, the skin and nails. From the psychological point of view, there are four hand shapes, these being , the Square or Practical Hand [EARTH];the Spatulate or Energetic Hand [FIRE];the Conic or Artistic Hand [WATER] ;and the Philosophical or Intellectual Hand [AIR].

CHIROMANCY represents the Palmar Regions, specifically the Major and Minor lines, their qualities and flow across your hand. Here we will examine depth, width, tone, and definition. These are like rivers and streams showing your journeys.

Next, we will look at THE MOUNTS (small mounds of flesh) which rise like mountains from the hand and represent your gifts or abilities.

DERMATOGLYPHICS represent the skin ridge patterns and your fingerprint patterns. On the fingertips they show psychological characteristics; on the palm, they reveal aspects of your personality, e.g., humour, seriousness, memory, etc.

CHIROGNOMY – THE OUTER FORM

Chirology, or Scientific Palmistry, comprises of Chirognomy (the Shape of Hands) and Chiromancy (The Palmar Regions).

Physically, or from a physiological perspective, the human hand is composed of Metacarpal bones, the Radial and Ulnar arteries, peripheral blood vessels, nerve endings, the skin formation, and nail structure. While Chirognomy is concerned with the structure and shape of the hands, Dermatoglyphics deal with skin ridge patterns, an example of which can be seen in the fingerprint records kept by the police.

CHIROMANCY – THE INNER FORM

This concerned with the Palmar Regions, as well as the mounts and lines on the hand. The colour, texture, and temperature of the skin metabolism, the width, depth, tone, and definition of the lines give great insight into a person's abilities, strengths, and weaknesses. Chirognomy deals with the character of people, and their outward consciousness of the world; whereas Chiromancy deals with their personality and psychology, as well as the inner workings of their lives, career, relationships, health, and chronology.

A person's left hand represents their origins, family, potential, and passive feminine strengths. It is also a record of their lives; similar to a library. A person's right hand represents their evolvement, will direction and orientation to the world; and a person's active masculine strengths. However, if your client is left-handed these qualities are reversed.

Left-handed people are imaginative, intuitive, and perceptive. They are often gifted in the fields of art and music, and many athletics or physical agility can be found to be one of their many traits. There are also many successful left-handed business people.

Right-handed people show reasoning abilities, logic, adaptability, and the capacity to learn. Most people from Europe, Australia, U.S.A, and Canada are right handed.

HAND TYPE CLASSIFICATION (REFER TO FIGURE ONE)

A   SQUARE/PRACTICAL HANDS – "I Serve" - EARTH

Description: Square palm with short fingers; thick, wide palms; coarse skin, along with few deep lines; square fingertips.

Key Words: Practical, reliable, conventional, trustworthy, loving food, the countryside. Traditional, distrustful of words. Cautious, reserved, seeking capable and down to earth partners, patient, tolerant, with excellent stamina. Although sometimes reserved, often useful with their hands, e.g., craftwork, tool making.

Career Orientations: Farming, engineering, building, horticulture, cooking, mining, sculpture, dancing, athletics (weight-lifting, boxing)

B   CONIC/EMOTIONAL HANDS - "I Feel" -WATER

Description: Oblong palm with narrow, tapering fingers; long, thin, narrow or rounded palms; beautiful skin; soft, elastic fingers; pointed tips.

Key Words: Sensitive, artistic, sympathetic, responsive, compassionate, emotional, fastidious, spiritual, versatile, fertile, musical.

Career Orientations: Nurses, doctors, artists, musicians, actors, nuns, athletics (swimming, running), counsellors, therapists, linguists.

C   PHILOSOPHICAL/INTELLECTUAL HANDS – "I Think" -AIR

Description: Square palm with long wide fingers. Short, wide palms; dry, delicate skin; long, broad fingers; rounded tips.

Key Words: Thoughtful, intellectual, unconventional, humorous, inventive, logical, impersonal, perceptive, quick-witted, diplomatic, critical.

Career Orientations: Scholars, diplomats, doctors, lawyers, politicians, broadcasters, entertainers, directors, teachers, inventors, professors, religious leaders.

D   SPATULATE/ENERGETIC HANDS - "I Act"-FIRE

Description: Oblong palm with short fingers; long, wide, thick palms; elastic, springy skin; short, spatulate fingers.

Key Words: Energetic, active, intuitive, impetuous, creative, enthusiastic, argumentative, inspired, restless, unconventional – The Pioneer.

Career Orientations: Soldiers, explorers, astronauts, engineers, authors, seers, chefs, pilots, travel couriers, sales managers, leaders in business & industry.

FIGURE ONE: HAND TYPE CLASSIFICATION

Philosophical Hands - Air
"I Think"

Spatulate Hands - Fire
"I Act"

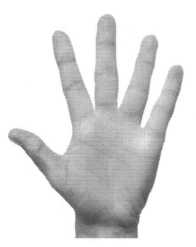
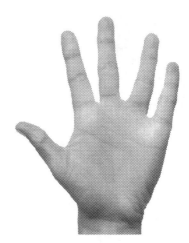

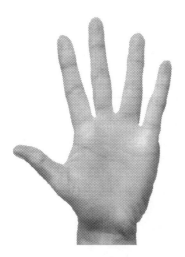
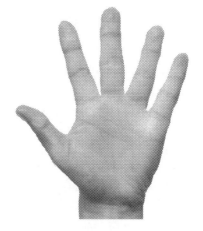

Conic Hands - Water
"I Feel"

Square Hands - Earth
"I Serve"

THE FINGERS AND THUMBS

Fingers represent our spheres of interests and our grasp of the Real World. They indicate our intellectual attributes and our conscious desires for self expression. The fingers are ruled by Planets as follows:

THUMB	=	MARS	-	Logic, Willpower and Direction in life
INDEX FINGER	=	JUPITER	-	Inspirations, Ambition, Creativity, Ego, Food & Money
MIDDLE FINGER	=	SATURN	-	Traditions, Science, Law, Ethics, Religious Institutions, Agriculture and Craftsmanship
RING FINGER	=	APOLLO	-	Music, Sports, Arts, Self-expression, Public offices
LITTLE FINGER	=	MERCURY	-	Communications, Electronics, Linguistics, Medicine, Sexuality and Children

THE THUMB – ETHER -SPIRIT

In Palmistry, the Thumb expresses the Energy of the Individual. In direct terms, it represents a person's willpower, decision-making abilities and passions.

There are three settings for the Thumb – lower, medial and high. The lower example indicates a person of strength, who has physical agility and may be drawn to sporting activities. The medial position is a balanced one, illustrating a sense of harmony between physical and mental pursuits. The higher setting is that of the aspirant, one who is idealistic and pursues intellectual stimulation. They may enjoy discussing art or music, or be attracted to the professions. However, they may be narrow minded and dogmatic.

There is great debate as to the ideal length of this digit. I ascertain that each phalange should be equal in length, indicating a balanced reasoning ability and the correct application of judgement, resulting in organisation.

The first or lower phalange of the thumb represents desire to create, the desire to act. This area is termed the Mount of Venus.

The second phalange shows reasoning ability. When full and waited this indicated diplomacy, tact and a desire to maximise the economy of energy expended. When over-long, this section causes the subject to be indecisive and to prefer to argue and debate matters, being incapable of acting. A short

phalange shows that the person will be impulsive, instinctively acting sometimes without any clear cut plan. A thick, wide middle phalange indicates an honest, direct approach to others. Diplomacy may be lacking! This person may deliberate rather than act and is not easily counselled.

The third phalange relates to the "fuel" of power divested in the thumb and thus refers to action. A long phalange herein tells of the subject's great determination, stamina and persistence. Thin, long phalanges indicate subtlety and great precision – an eye surgeon could have such a thumb to enhance the accuracy and deftness their profession requires of them.

Very thin nail phalanges show the strategist, one who succeeds with apparently little effort.

Square tipped thumbs are practical and often found on the palms of engineers. There is also present a love of the truth and an inherent desire for justice.

Spatulate thumbs are the tool of the craftsman – painters, sculptors and musicians often have this formation.

Clubbed thumbs used to be considered to indicate a confused of frustrated nature. In past times called "The Murderers' Thumb", such melodramatic terminology is inappropriate and misleading. The true meaning is that these people are deficient in the actuation of their willpower at an instinctive level. Whilst this may also be true of criminals, I have met many charming and capable people with this feature! However, I believe this often indicates hardship and inner turmoil. Anger management is always necessary!

People with such formations often lack sufficient control of their will power and emotions and may be drawn towards excesses. Once I found this sign on the hand of a charming man who excelled in professional career but unfortunately involved himself in pornography and paedeophilia. However this is not always the case and when found only on the left hand may only indicate an obsessive and obtuse individual.

Note the flexibility of the joints. Great flexibility of the thumb tip is a certain indication of the spendthrift or gambler and shows a lack is of perseverance. However, such individuals quickly adapt to the changing circumstances of home and career. A fixed joint indicates stubbornness.

Finally note if the upper phalange is held into the palm or curves outwards. A curved phalange indicates a generous nature, one who gives to others and may take up a cause on their behalf. A close-held thumb indicates a self-indulgent nature but may also be interpreted as cautious or reserved.

INDEX-FINGER – JUPITER - WATER

Representing ego and self-awareness; our desire to express ourselves, expand our abilities, to exhibit our talents.

This finger should reach to the bottom of the nail of the Middle Finger. People with longer fingers attain to positions of leadership, e.g. directors, professors or university teachers.

A short finger indicates lack of confidence and the inability to assert will- power. When the top phalange is short, a marked sense of inferiority may be present.

The lower jupiterian phalange, when full, illustrates a person who likes good food and material luxuries. Such a person is independent but is sensitive to their environment – they like to choose their conditions of work. Short, narrow phalanges indicate hardships, perhaps poverty or a repressed childhood.

A good second phalange shows the ability to organise; a man may be a D.I.Y enthusiast, a woman may have excellent secretarial or managerial abilities. Often men with large phalanges have business abilities or an aptitude for accounts or economics. When short, a person may not make the best of their opportunities or remain in a subordinate position. A long upper phalange indicates nobility, idealism and aspiration and is the hallmark of a person in authority. Diplomats, Politicians and Religious leaders often have such a phalange. However, when rounded, dominance and an overbearing nature may be apparent.

The finger should be straight. When bent inward onto the second finger this indicates sacrifices to cause, or loyalty to family ties.

SECOND FINGER – SATURN - EARTH

This finger in its highest form represents science, law, philosophy (especially morality) and administration. Generally, it shows how a person relates to society and responsibilities and is intimately concerned with career prospects and social position. Saturn the Stabiliser rules it.

An overly long finger indicates a reserved and studious individual, perhaps over-cautious, but responsible. Narrow mindedness may prevail. Short fingers indicate a rebellious nature or a person unable to settle down. Extremely short fingers are the hallmark of the professional criminal.

Long base phalanges indicate gifts in crafts, botany, farming or archaeology. The strong second phalange indicates executive ability, being the hallmark of the lawyer, doctor and those who achieve management positions in private or public offices.

A short middle phalange shows impatience, irresponsibility and a lack of interest in attaining to positions of authority. A well-proportioned nail phalange indicates intellectual ability in the fields of law, science and art – however this person will demand respect and may not be modest about their attributes.

A straight finger shows self-restraint and a poised person. If found leaning towards Apollo (ring finger), job satisfaction and not financial reward is the primary career motive.

A square tip to this finger is preferable, depicting instinctive, practical judgement.

A flexible nail phalange indicates intuitive or psychic abilities; if the whole finger is flexible, a person may be gullible or self-deceptive. Where the top finger joint is knotted, i.e. bulges out, this is the sign of the philosopher, deep thinker and writer!

THIRD FINGER – APOLLO - FIRE

This finger represents creative expression and an emotional motivation towards happiness. Apollo was the Sun God and bestowed musical and artistic gifts upon followers. Whereas the index finger relates to private ambitions, the third finger relates to public life. In my experience, a long finger is the hallmark of the moral person, being a sign of perfectionism, bestowing gifts of oratory (as on the hands of teachers and salespeople) of creative gifts (as on the hands of artists, musicians and dancers).

The top of the finger should be level with the middle of the upper phalange of Saturn (middle finger). A short finger shows an adventurous soul, a pioneer or gambler.

A long base phalange shows a competent gardener or decorator or possibly a sculptor and maybe a painter or musician. A short phalange indicates frustrations, lack of comfort or a detrimental environment. A long middle phalange shows selectivity of creative pursuits – the specialist. A precision toolmaker or fashion designer may have this formation; they use economy and like objects to be functional. A long nail phalange is the sign of the art historian, composer or graphic designer. They appreciate the exactness of colour, tone or the importance of a correct brush stroke.

Apollo fingers should be straight. When they lean towards Saturn (middle finger) this indicates a sense of duty and such people may be anxious to please parents. A square tip to the nail phalange shows a good eye for proportions. A knotted second joint indicates a tidy person with a love of order. An overly long finger indicates perfectionism – the sign of a critic.

FOURTH FINGER –MERCURY - AIR

In proportion, this finger should come half way up to the nail phalange of the Apollo finger (ring finger). Long fingers show personal charisma, sex appeal and excellent power of oratory or the capacity for abstract thought. A short finger denotes quick wittedness and sudden temper.

The base phalange rules money. A thick phalange indicates a desire to collect. Long second phalanges are the mark of the accountant, linguist or scientist (perhaps a doctor). Short second phalanges are symptoms of confusion of spendthrift nature. A good nail phalange shows gifts of speech and an intuitive understanding of others.

However, when long and bent towards Apollo a person may deceive; when curved towards the palm indicates a businessperson or a talent for theft.

A wide angled finger of Mercury indicates independence and an outspoken nature. Close held fingers are traditional or modest. A low set finger indicates difficulties in childhood and such people hate criticism and tend to be cautious in words and action. Often "dropped" little fingers show immaturity and naïveté. However, on a positive note, these people often get on well with children and animals because they are playful and sensitive. Flexible fingers show a retentive memory.

SPACING BETWEEN THE FINGERS

GENERAL GUIDELINES

Wide spacing between fingers shows many diverse interests in life (often found on the hands of extroverts).

Narrow spacing between fingers shows the focusing-in of the attention on specialised interests (often found on the hands of introverts).

When spacing is extreme, there is a tendency to compartmentalise or "parcel-out" life experiences. Often either information or money slips easily through these people's hands.

Conversely, where the fingers are tightly held together and curl in to the palm, great caution, obedience and a strict control of self-expression is indicated. In my experience such individuals are tense and wary of strangers; conditions brought about by traumatic experiences, hardships and stress. These people are often the "victim of circumstances". I am especially caring and sympathetic towards them – any form of criticism may cause distress.

THE SETTINGS OF THE FINGERS

As a rule, high set fingers show a sense of security and position with society. Low set fingers show insecurity and loss of esteem either personally or professionally.

INDEX FINGER

HIGH SET - Egotism, ambition, domination – "Hallmark of The Leader".

LOW SET - Lack of faith, hopelessness, and loss of esteem – "The Victim".

MIDDLE FINGER

HIGH SET - Responsibility, duty, honour – "Conventional Respect".

LOW SET - Immorality, anarchy, loss of social position – "The Rebel".

THIRD FINGER

HIGH SET - Perfectionism, public service – "Creative Expression".

LOW SET - Gambling, lust – "The Fraud and Confidence Trickster".

FOURTH FINGER

HIGH SET - Charisma, sex appeal – "The Confident Communicator".

LOW SET –Vunerability, insecurity, naïveté –"Inferiority Complex ".

FINGERTIP SHAPES

The fingertips express the way we communicate our ideas to others. In other words, they represent the energy of self-expression.

Square/Practical Tip

Cautious, shy, reserved in the use of spoken or written words. Traditional, methodical, conventional and obedient in public or private situations.

Intellectual/Philosophical Tip

Reasoning, discrimination, thoughtful, possessing mental dexterity, often taking enjoyment in debating. Development of strong psychological or philosophical beliefs in their personal and public lives.

Conic/EmotionalTip

Focused, inspired, sensitive, receptive to use of language. Spiritual, intuitive, refined and graceful in public and private life.

Spatulate/Energetic Tip

Aspiring, visionary, dynamic, fervent in their use of language. Idealistic, ardent, sometimes fanatical in their views, preferring action to words.

CHIROLOGY

MAJOR LINES OF THE PALM (REFER TO FIGURE TWO)

Lines on the hand indicate a person's use of energy, being a representation of an individual's conscious and unconscious drives, mental and emotional attributes. There are four major lines being the MENTAL LINE, the EMOTIVE LINE, the LINE OF VITALITY and the CREATIVE LINE. The following is a table of attributes:

LINE FORMATION	RULERSHIP	ATTRIBUTES
LINE OF VITALITY (The Life Line)	EARTH	Representing the vital energy of the individual, their health, sustaining faculty, physical power and consciousness of TIME
LINE OF EMOTIONS (The Heart Line)	MOON	Representing intensity, feelings, emotions, intuition, circulatory system and consciousness of CHANGE
LINE OF MENTALITY (The Head Line)	MERCURY	Representing aspirations, discrimination, intellectual abilities and reasoning faculties, plus SELF-AWARENESS.
LINE OF CREATIVITY (Apollo)	SUN	Representing stability, self-assertion, ego, the arts and crafts, the metabolism of a person and consciousness of quality in THE FIVE SENSES

Vitality Line	=	SOLID	-	FOUNDATION	-	Physical World
Emotional Line	=	FLUID	-	ADAPTATION	-	Intuitive World
Mental Line	=	GASEOUS	-	AWARENESS	-	Communicative World
Creative Line	=	ATOMIC	-	EVOLUTIONARY	-	Energetic World

LINE OF VITALITY (LIFE LINE) - EARTH

This line encompasses the area of the mount of Venus, commencing under the Mount of Jupiter and above the area termed Lower Mars. It represents one's external vitality. The Line of mercury governs a person's Internal Metabolism.

A common mistake among students is to consider that a broken Life Line or short one indicates a short or unhealthy life. That is not true. In most cases, a line will join with the Fate Line indicating a major change in lifestyle such as emigration, a career move or sometimes a marriage. It is only when the Inner Life of Mars (running inside the Life Line parallel to it) is broken that chronic illness is indicated. A well-placed line is not tied to any other but gently curves round the palm to end below the Mount of Venus. It should give space to the Mount. Herein it indicates an expansive and generous nature, an optimist who will have many spheres of interest; these may be indicated by the size and quality of the Mount of Venus.

A line tied to the Head Line for 1 inch before the Life Line leaves it is an indication that a person's childhood may have been dominated by parental interference; when set low onto the Mount of Lower Mars courage has been sought.

A line commencing high on Jupiter or sending a Line to Jupiter illustrates a person's ambitions.

A line that breaks and has a parallel line, which continues on course, shows that a person has taken on a completely different lifestyle. Stress Lines may cut across the Vitality Line laterally at intervals; people or events that affect a person's life cause these.

The line will continue until the Mount of Neptune; here it may branch or be crossed by the Health Line. A line branching towards Luna indicates a person who is restless and may travel or emigrate (look for travel lines on Luna). When curving under the Mount of Venus a person will love their home and probably die in the country to which they are born.

Terminations in the Vitality Line vary. A tasselled end means a dissipation of life. It is quite common for the Line of Mercury to cross the Life Line. This indicates internal ailments. Chronology relating to this line will be shown in the latter part of this course. Note, if a person's Lifeline is close-held to the Mount of Venus, this indicates a cautious nature; possibly a narrow-minded person or one who sacrifices much for one cause. A reserved, shy or frugal nature is often shown.

Finally, it is important to remember that the Vitality Line is linked metaphorically to all other major lines and reflects these lines.

LINE OF EMOTIONS (HEART LINE) - WATER

This line crosses the palm underneath the fingers, starting at the edge of the hand under the Mount of Mercury. The line represents a person's emotional response to life.

A balance person's line will flow across the hand terminating between the ringers of Jupiter and Apollo. This line shows a harmonious nature and a practical and caring response to others.

The HIGH SET HEART LINE indicates one who is demonstrative in their relationships. They will shout, scream, passionately debate and are sensual in their lovemaking.

The LOW SET HEART LINE indicates the opposite, namely one who is undemonstrative and represses their emotions. They will pout, moan and sulk, being calm, cool and rational, with a mental response to lovemaking.

In partnership matter, similar Heart Lines show compatibility.

Often a Line also flows on to the Mount of Jupiter. This shows idealism and is often found on the hands of humanitarians, being a sign of philanthropy. These people love fervently and with generosity.

When a line descends and touches or joins the Vitality Line this is a sign of compassion, a life of sacrifice or a person relying on courage to maintain stability (this person will hide their emotions).

Lines rising onto <u>Mercury</u> are called Sympathy Lines or Medical Stigmata. They indicate great compassion and are vocational lines, e.g. counsellors, healers, therapists, doctors, nurses or vets.

Often people have a Girdle of Venus; this indicated added intensity of emotions, sensitivity, sensuality, dreams and fantasies – a secret world.

Dots on the Heart Line often indicate heart attacks and islands show respiratory problems. In general, from a health perspective, the Heart Line relates to the circulatory system.

LINE OF MENTALITY (HEADLINE) -AIR

This line crosses the palm, starting from under the thumb and below the Mount of Jupiter and ending at some point on the Mount of Luna, parallel to the Line of Emotions. This line represents our thoughts and reasoning power and mental approach to life – discrimination.

It is often tied to the LifeLines; herein it shows a person sensitive to the needs of their family – a period of dependency. A third party influences one, ususally parents or teachers.

When the line runs straight across the palm, this indicates a practical and <u>objective</u> mentality – this is called the HIGH SET HEADLINE. This person will be logical, reasoning, pragmatic, or scientific. A long Line shows psychological understanding. The mentality rules over the emotions.

A line that sweeps down toward Luna is <u>subjective;</u> this person will probably be imaginative, artistic, and intuitive – this is called the LOW SET HEADLINE. The emotions rule over thinking.

A line descending to Lower Luna indicates a person with latent psychic ability. Conversely, however, this person may be a dreamer or at worst, a depressive manic.

A line that forks at the end with one branch descending slightly have been called a Writers' Fork. "Imagination produces novels of worth." However, painters or composers may also have this sign.

Lines that ascend towards the Line of Emotions indicate aspirations or mental gifts. Lines descending from this line indicate mental anxieties or the setback of a person's projects or careers.

The Line's attributes may be better understood when read in conjunction with the nail phalanges of the fingers, which represent mentality.

A long mental line shows a good memory, intelligence, perception, thoughtfulness, analytical, practical abilities – a person capable of organising and solving problems. When stretching to the edge of the palm, proficiency in psychology or exceptional mental dexterity may be present.

Short lines illustrate an impetuous, impulsive, active person, seeking challenges and experiences. Quick thinkers; these people respond to energy situations fast and are instinctive when executing plans.

Very short lines (often found on Practical Hands); they show a simplistic nature.

I have discovered that this line relates to the skeletal system so that where a line is broken, a back problem is often indicated.

<u>LINE OF CREATIVITY</u> (THE APOLLO LINE) -FIRE

This Line of Creativity may commence at any point on the lower palm, but its destination is the Mount under the finger of Apollo. It represents a person's aspirations and is often related to careers. When the line commences on the Mount of Luna, a career in the public eye is indicated, e.g., in service to the public (Civil Service, advertising, journalism).

When it commences from the Life Line or within it, this illustrates a person whose career is either self-made or influenced by the family.

The Line may not appear until it is above the Line of Emotions. Herein it represents hard work and achievement later in life, possibly through an interest.

A series of line underneath Apollo indicate versatility and a person's social standing. They will never be without friends or money for they are capable of adapting to various conditions.

A line terminated towards Mercury indicates a flair for business; when found towards Saturn, the person has a great sense of responsibility and duty towards their work, e.g., a company man or devoted secretary.

A line starting in the Higher Region of Luna, on the Percussion, and curving towards Apollo is a sign of business intuition; money will be easily generated, and such a person may inherit wealth.

When the line is absent, this indicates a perfectionist; someone never satisfied with his or her achievements.

THE LINE OF HEALTH (INTERNAL MEDICAL LINE) -AIR

The Health Line represents the internal health of a person and is the mirror of the Life Line, which represents external health.

When absent, the Health Line shows unusually robust health. Equally, a straight unbroken line shows good health. Broken lines show delicacy in health matters.

Where the line cuts into the Life Line, it shows the need to look after one's health, being an indicator of a dysfunction in the internal organs.

Like most Lines, the Life Line has "protector lines" providing support. Only when the Inner Line of Mars (turning parallel to the Life Line, but inside it) is broken that is when a chronic ill health shown.

Islands in these line show periods of ill health. Dots in the Line show traumas or shocks. It is important to remember that the Health Line is <u>only one</u> of the indicators in health matters.

THE LINE OF STABILITY (THE FATE LINE) - EARTH

The Fate Line, as it is traditionally termed, indicates the manifestation of the will to provide a direction in life. Therefore, we are talking about a person's identity; a sense of worth, feelings of security and stability, and their progress through life.

A well-formed line commencing on the Mount of Neptune proceeding up the palm unbroken and deep is a sure sign of success in the career. I call this the "Vocational Line" because these people have a sense of dedication and purpose.

When starting from within the Life Line, family influence in the choice of working life is shown. Proceeding from the Life Line itself is often the sign of the self-made careerist. Beginning from the Mount of Luna is an excellent position for anyone serving the public; this indicates that success depends on diplomacy. Often those in the public eye, especially actors and creative people, have this line feature.

Breaks in the line show career changes. If the line is made up of many small lines, this is a sign of great instability both personally and professionally, which is always found on the hands of those who frequently change jobs as well as being the hallmark of a gambler and risk-taker!

The Fate Line is the barometer of change and therefore has great significance when dealing with health matters. It also is an ideal Line on which to judge the timing of events (CHRONOLOGY), e.g., when you move house. We will deal with these matters separately in later chapters.

FIGURE TWO: MAJOR LINES OF THE PALM

A - Life Line   B - Heart Line
C - Head Line   D - Line of Creativity
E - Health Line   F - Fate Line
G - Partnership Line   H - Children

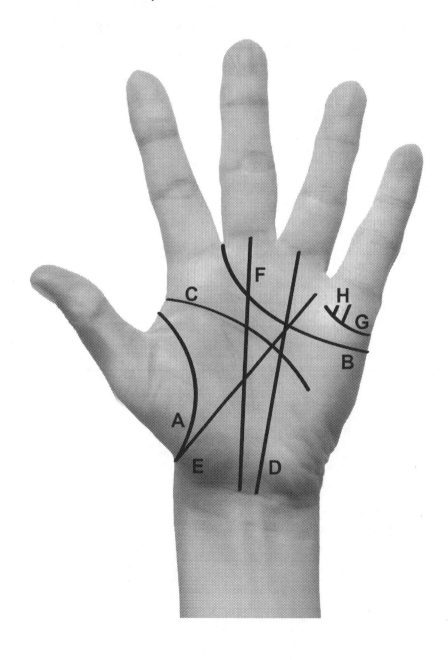

MINOR LINES OF THE PALM (REFER TO FIGURE THREE)

VIA LASCIVIA

This encompasses the Area of Neptune, from Luna to Venus, at the base of the palm. This line reflects the Girdle of Venus and relates to not emotional but physical sensitivity.

Alcohol, drugs, and risks should be avoided by the owner of this line. It represents sensitivity, allergies, anorexia, hypochondria or addictions.

THE GIRDLE OF VENUS (METABOLIC, EMOTIONAL HEALTH LINE)

When well-formed, this indicates a psychologically well-balanced person, sensitive with deep emotions.

When broken it indicates intensity, dreams, fantasies, and dramatic tendencies, e.g., role-playing.

Where one section of this Line from the base of the Finger of Apollo detaches itself and travels through the Heart and Head Lines touching the Life Line, this is one of the indicators of bisexuality or homosexuality. In this aspect, fantasy has been transformed into real life! It is important as a palmist to be sensitive to people's rights as human beings to choose their own sexual orientation. This is why I have decided in this edition to rename the Marriage Line as the Partnership Line to reflect these individual preferences.

If the lines are stretched across the hand towards the Partnership Line, these people often tend to get suspicious or jealousy is present.

RING OF SOLOMON

A curved line indicates this sign underneath the index finger. This illustrates a person who prefers to work in a group. It may also show a person who is interested in learning.

A HIGH SET RING shows intuitive psychic abilities or an interest in the occult or philosophy.

A MIDDLE SET RING shows an understanding of psychology and is often accompanied by insight.

A LOW SET RING shows insight into practical matters, e.g., crafts.

When present on both hands, the ability to teach or train others will be present, especially where there is a Teachers' Square on the Mount of Jupiter.

Ring of Saturn

This encompasses the Mount of Saturn. This is often an indicator of a melancholic personality ,wherein often due to traumas,a person can become self destructive,or suffer from moods and depression.

Partnership Lines

This appears as a horizontal line or lines under the finger of Mercury. When straight it indicates a harmonious love life.

When curved downwards, it indicates disappointments in love or that the loving partner may die before you do! When forked at the end, a separation or divorce is a possibility.

Lines rising vertically from this line show children. Thin lines indicate female children and thick lines, indicate male children. Crosses on these lines show accidents to children.

SPECIAL NOTE: To interpret this Line accurately, we should be aware of two critical factors. First, the Line is principally concerned with love and affection. However, I have met single people, elderly women, and many other people who have possessed this Line but <u>never got</u> married. Some of these people love animals, e.g., a cat or dog, adopt children or express affection in different ways. Therefore, it is true to say that in reality, the line represents the object of one's affections.

Secondly, the number of Lines appearing on the palm is no certain indicator of partnership. Love is the most important thing in life, and without which fulfilment, it may be elusive.

The Quality of Lines

Lines may end in many ways. If they simply fade out, this shows a person's energy in that field, e.g., Mentality or Emotionality, has come to its natural end. Crosses indicate accidents and stars indicate a violent dispersal of energy.

A line ending with an island shows that confusion and frustration are present. Dots show shocks – on Head Line mental trauma; on the Heart Line, emotional upsets or heart attacks.

Note: figures relating to line endings.

FIGURE THREE: MINOR LINES OF THE PALM

A - Bar Lines   B - Hyper Striations
C - Vertical Lines   D - Medical Stigmata
E - Teacher's Square   F - Line of Intuition
G - Via Lascivia   H - The Ring of Solomon
I - Girdle of Venus

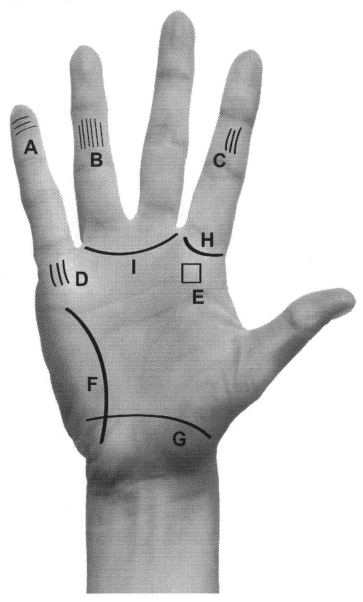

FIGURE FOUR: CHRONOLOGY

The palm can be dated by using a number of references. These are better illustrated pictorially. In general, lines reflect one another, and therefore it is important to notice and look at the Major Lines and notice that when events occue they are mirrored in other lines.

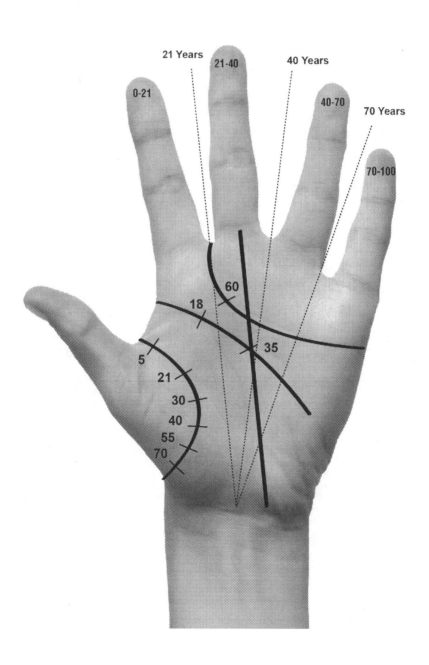

SKIN RIDGE PATTERNS

This area of study is called DERMATOGLYPHICS. Most people these days have heard of the Ancient Egyptians and the depictions of their lives visually and symbolically in the Pyramids.

Skin Ridge Patterns are the blueprints (like a photographic negative) of the hands. Genetically, people in family groups who are blood-related will have similar fingerprint patterns.

The Palmar Skin Ridge Patterns show personality and social indicators. The FingerPrint Patterns show psychological orientation. Please now refer to the Skin Ridge Diagram below that shows the position and meanings of these patterns.

FINGERPRINT PATTERNS

 Practical Print Pattern - *Simple Arches*

 Energetic Print Pattern - *Extended Arches*

 Emotional Print Pattern - *Loops*

 Mental Print Pattern - *Concentric Circles*

FIGURE FIVE: DERMATOGLYPHICS
Skin Ridge Patterns

A - Raja Loop *(Public Service)*   B - Loop of Serious Intent
C - Loop of Humour   D - Line of Courage
E - Loop of Reason   F - Loop of Nature
G - Psychic Abilities   H - Loop of Vision
I - Loop of Instinct   J - Loop of Music *(The Bee-sting)*

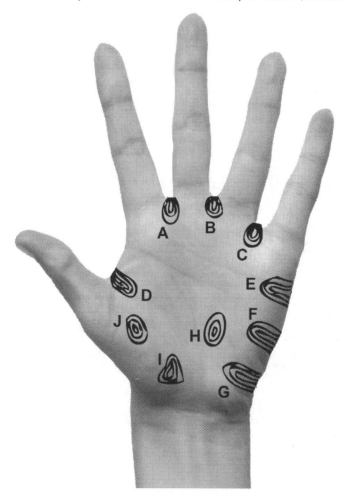

SKIN TYPES

There are four basic skin types. An interesting fact is that people can, for instance, have a Conic or Emotional hand type but have the Energetic skin type. With skin, we are concerned with the <u>quality</u> of life, experiences and specifically relationships.

ENERGETIC SKIN TYPE -FIRE

Energetic skin type is relatively coarse. It has wide pores and indicates response to life of an active kind. It has been, in my experience, likely that at least two fingerprint patterns will also have Whorl formations.

EMOTIONAL SKIN TYPE- WATER

Emotional skin type is extremely fine and silky and also has small pores. This indicates a person who will have a sensitive response to life. The memory may be good, and there is a strong possibility that the person will have many thin lines on the hand.

INTELLECTUAL SKIN TYPE- AIR

Intellectual skin type is also a fine skin, but the hand will probably be more rounded and plump. There will be fewer lines on the palm, and the person will have a rational response to life.

PRACTICAL SKIN TYPE –EARTH

Practical skin type is very coarse and thick. A person with this skin has a potentially practical approach to life. There may be a few lines. The hand may also have calluses and rough knuckle formations.

THE MOUNTS OF THE PALM

Mounts on the palm are reservoirs of energy. They represent quality and are found underneath the digits and at the side of the palm.

The following Major Mounts appear on the palm – Venus, Jupiter, Saturn, Apollo, Mercury, Luna; and also Minor Mounts – Upper Mars, Lower Mars, Neptune.

There is an apice in the centre of each Mount, which forms a tri-radius of lines around it. Mounts may be central or displaced.

MOUNT OF JUPITER

When centrally placed, this Mount represents dignity, self-respect, and moral convictions. When displaced towards Saturn, a persons' duty to family or society is shown. Displacement towards the thumb indicates a lack of caution, an adventurous nature, but one inclined towards delinquency or recklessness.

MOUNT OF SATURN

When centrally placed, the Mount indicates common-sense and a good understanding of financial values. Displaced towards Apollo suggests a lack of caution in dealing with money. When the Mount is low set, interest in land-owning is shown.

MOUNT OF APOLLO

A well placed Mount is a good sign for the practical artist who will show instinctive, creative expression. When looped towards the Line of Emotions it indicates a compassionate nature and one who may love animals or little children.

MOUNT OF MERCURY

A person with a centrally placed apice will have a love for words: verbal expression or literature. Such a person may simply like crossword puzzles or enjoy reading historical biographies. When it leans towards Apollo, a person may be gifted with words, e.g., a writer.

MOUNT OF VENUS

The Mount of Venus represents harmony, a sense of beauty and physical passion. When high, it shows a well-adapted sense of love. Over-full shows voluptuousness, while under-developed shows coldness. Apices on hands are rare and show collective memory and strong ties between religion and the person – a code of living.

MOUNT OF NEPTUNE

The Mount symbolises the Earth and relates to unconscious desires and a persons' psyche. A well-developed Mount may indicate awareness and good memory with an active subconscious mind.

MOUNT OF LUNA

An apex here indicates a selfless worker for who recognition does not come. The Mount represents the subconscious and imaginative side of a persons' nature. When this area is rounded, a gift of Spiritual Healing may be apparent (The Creative Curve).

FIGURE SIX: THE MOUNTS

The Mounts	Talents
A - Mount of Mercury	Speech, Singing, Linguistics
B - Mount of Apollo	Arts, Crafts, Management
C - Mount of Saturn	Science, Skills, Administration
D - Mount of Jupiter	Power, Religion, Politics
E - Lower Mars	Courage, Gambling
F - Mount of Venus	Love, Passion, Music
G - Mount of Neptune	Subconscious talents
H - Mount of Luna	Imagination
I - Upper Mars	Inner strength
J - Mount of Mars	Area of life activity

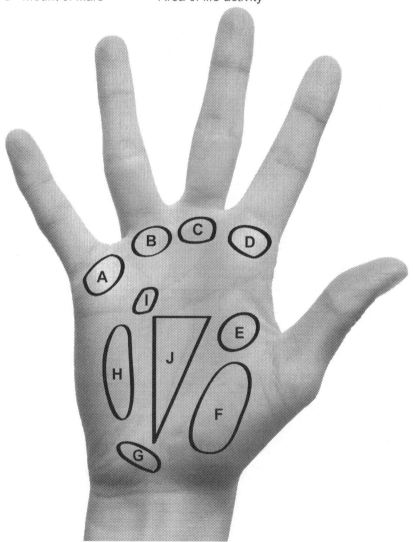

LOVE AND SEXUALITY IN THE HANDS

Like Astrology, Palmistry can be used to interpret in a compatibility system similar to Synastry to determine Hand-Chart harmonies.

HAND-TYPE MATCHING CHARACTERISTICS

A.   Square/Practical Hands

LOVE – Traditional family value predominate. Finding a capable, down to earth partner, getting married, having children, is of paramount importance. Stability, security, and support are vital.

SEXUALITY – Sensual, hedonistic, strong physical lust and stamina combined with caution, distrust of words and undemonstrative love. Loyalty, trust, and devotion are demanded.

B.   Conical/Emotional Hands

LOVE – Sympathetic, compassionate, caring values where emotions are easily expressed and desired. Intuitive and spiritual, physical beauty or shared ideals are essential. Fertile, loving and unselfish, positive and negative emotions can join.

SEXUALITY – Flexible, nubile, imaginative, soft and tactile, relaxed, steamy. Prolonged lovemaking is preferred.

C.   Philosophical/Mental Hands

LOVE – Partnerships, shared beliefs, humour and exciting locations. Express versatility and intellectual agreement. Role-playing and creativity make for stimulating, flexible relationships.

SEXUALITY – Inventive, dramatic, imaginative, lovemaking may be like a game of physical chess or in an unusual location, e.g. the "mile high club."

D.   Energetic/Spatulate Hands

LOVE – Impulsive, intense, enthusiastic lovemaking, which combine physical and intellectual needs. Active, aggressive, love is conquest, an ecstatic battle.

SEXUALITY – Passionate, sensuous, sex is quick and energetic, fast and impetuous. Anytime, anyway, anyhow, we want it <u>now</u>!

COMPATIBILITY

Square/Practical	Square/Practical	Harmonious	Compatible
Square/Practical	Conic/Emotional	Harmonious	Compatible
Square/Practical	Spatulate/Energetic	Challenging	Incompatible
Square/Practical	Philosophical/Mental	Challenging	Incompatible
Conic/Emotional	Square/Practical	Harmonious	Compatible
Conic/Emotional	Conic/Emotional	Harmonious	Compatible
Conic/Emotional	Philosophical/Mental	Challenging	Incompatible
Conic/Emotional	Spatulate/Energetic	Challenging	Incompatible
Philosophical/Mental	Square/Practical	Challenging	Incompatible
Philosophical/Mental	Conic/Emotional	Challenging	Incompatible
Philosophical/Mental	Philosophical/Mental	Harmonious	Compatible
Philosophical/Mental	Spatulate/Energetic	Harmonious	Compatible
Spatulate/Energetic	Square/Practical	Challenging	Incompatible
Spatulate/Energetic	Conic/Emotional	Challenging	Incompatible
Spatulate/Energetic	Philosophical/Mental	Harmonious	Compatible
Spatulate/Energetic	Spatulate/Energetic	Harmonious	Compatible

As in Astrology, people may be attracted to their opposite. Also, the myriad of palmar features should be considered to determine compatibility, especially the Heart Lines.

IN-DEPTH ANALYSIS

Like in Astrology, where not only the Zodiac Sign but also all of the birth charts are compared, so in Palmistry Counselling we look at the fingers and thumbs, skin ridge patterns, the Mounts, major and minor lines to determine definite positive and negative traits.

However, as this is rather complex, these matters will be given space in my Advanced Professional Palmistry Counsellors Book ,published in 2019.

Meanwhile, why not try creating your own hand charts as a reference tool?

EQUIPMENT FOR THE PALMIST

A large magnifying glass is essential to read palmar features in detail, as is a ruler to measure hand shapes, dimensions of the fingers and major lines. It is invaluable when measuring the Fate Line to determine the timing of events.

GLOSSARY OF TERMS

TERMS

Chirology	- the analytical study of hands
Chirognomy	- the study of the shape of the hands
Chiromancy	- the study of the Palmar Region
Hermetic	- appertaining to the Ancient Philosophy of Creation
Karma	- the Laws of Cause and Effect
Macrocosm	- Mankind observed as a component manifestation of Divine Consciousness
Microcosm	- the manifestation in human consciousness of external Cosmic phenomena
Ontology	- the study of the essence of being
Palmistry	- the art of Hand Divination – fortune telling

OTHER MISCELLANEOUS LINES

islands indicate disillusionment

bars and dots indicate barriers and shocks

tassels indicate dissipation of energy

wavy lines show vacillation

vertical lines show activity

horizontal lines show inhibitions

curved lines within the Life Line are influence lines,

Being parents or loved ones reinforcing a person's energy

MISCELLANEOUS PALMAR FEATURES

Islands		- periods of confusion or disillusionment
Dots		- shocks/traumas either physical or psychological
Wavy Lines		- vacillation, indecision, procrastination, hesitancy
Crosses		- setbacks
Stars		- violence, great trauma, e.g. nervous breakdowns
Squares		- protection, safety, preservation from harm
Triangles		- good fortune, success
Forks		- division of energies or separation e.g. divorce
Breaks		- change of direction for good or ill
Bars		- inhibitions, restraints, blocks
Grilles		- struggle, lack of progress

FEATURES ON FINGERS AND THEIR PHALANGES

Striations (vertical lines)	| | |	- talents, skills, abilities
Hyper-Striations (many Striations)	|||||	- stress, overwork
Bars	===	- inhibitions, blocks to achievement

MEANINGS OF FINGER PHALANGES

Base Phalanges	- practical, down-to-earth skills and abilities
Middle Phalanges	-executive, organisation, management skills
Top Phalanges	- mental or spiritual abilities e.g. politics/clairvoyance

SUGGESTED RECOMMENDED BOOKS TO READ

* = Good : ** = Important : *** = Excellent (the best!)

A.	Any books by Cheiro, the famous Palmist	*
B.	Annals of Human Genetics by Sir Francis Galton (EUGENICS)	**
C.	The Human Hand, the Living Symbol of Noel Jacquin	***
D.	Hands and Faces by Mrs Katherine Ashton	*
E.	The Science of Hand Reading Simplified by K.C. Sen	**
F	Palmistry Made Easy by Johnny Fincham	**
G.	The Hand in Psychological Diagnosis by C. Wolfe	***
H.	The Human Hand by Sir Charles Bell	*
I.	Laws of Scientific Hand Reading by W. Benham	***
J.	The Palmistry Work-Book by Nathaniel Altman	**
K	Life Prints by Richard Unger	**
L.	The Theory of Metaphysical Influence by N. Jacquin	
M.	Studies in Hand Readings by N. Jacquin	
N.	How to Read Hands by Lori Reid ***	

Many excellent books are out of print. Seek out a good specialist second-hand bookshop.

John Harrison is the Founder of The Profession of Palmistry Counselling.

YOUR FIRST PALMISTRY READING

Ok, so now is the time to put knowledge into practice. Choose a friend or someone you feel comfortable with and try to make this a "fun exercise," a light-hearted experience.

SETTING THE SCENE

Relax. Do some meditation. Clear your thoughts and concentrate on the other person sending them thoughts of sympathy and understanding.

Sit in a well-lit room that is warm and pleasant. Light a candle, play soft music or light incense if you are both happy with this. We are trying to create an ambiance and a welcoming atmosphere.

LET'S GO FOR IT!

Gently take both of your friend's hands in yours. Close your eyes and use your intuition. How is this person feeling now?

After a few moments open your eyes and spend 3-5 minutes looking at their hands. Notice the shape of their hands, the Major and Minor lines. Take up your magnifying glass and closely inspect the fingerprint patterns. Look at the Mounts and finally the skin ridge patterns.

Think simple thoughts, e.g., are these large or small hands? Are they smooth or rough to the touch? Are there a few lines or many lines? Are the fingers long or short, widespread or closely held? Are the lines strong and unbroken or thin and fragile? Are the fingerprints all the same type or different? Now feel the Mounts and decide which are the best developed; these will show social skills. Are the Mounts fleshy or flat and hard? Are there any skin ridge symbols on these hands, e.g., Loop of Humour or Loop of Seriousness?

BEGINNING YOUR READING – Feeling nervous? Me too!!!

So the first thing to decide upon is the hand shape. Start by asking yourself whether the fingers are long or short relative to the length of the palm. If short, your friend has either Practical or Spatulate hands; if long, either Conic or Intellectual hands. The difference between the two types of short fingered hands is that the Practical hand is square, e.g., just as long as it is wide. The difference

between the Conic and Intellectual hand is that the Conic hand is narrow or thin with long tapering fingers. Refer to your notes and state the indication for the hand type.

Now, look at the fingers and thumbs. Pay special attention at the proportions of these, e.g. long, short, thick or thin. We now need to look at the fingerprints, which will give a unique insight into the mind of our friend, e.g. sociable, idealistic, individualistic, enthusiastic and energetic, imaginative. Make your interpretation of the thumb followed by each finger in succession. Longer fingers and thumbs show a greater <u>range</u> of ability. Shorter ones show limits to ability.

Next, we come to the palm itself and the lines. Begin with the Life Line. If long and unbroken this will show an active life with an expectancy of 75 or more. A short or broken line shows change and the need to take care of the health.

The Head Line is now analysed. Long or short, straight (high set) or curved (low set). Refer to your notes.

The Heart Line follows this. Long, ending between the Index and Second fingers? They are demonstrative with affections and emotionally responsive. Short or lower set? They are practical, independent and self-reliant.

The Fate line – a long unbroken line shows an excellent career. Where broken, changes are apparent.

Now after looking at the Health line, proceed to look at all the Minor lines, e.g., partnerships, Girdle of Venus, Ring of Solomon, etc.

Lastly, we look at the skin ridge patterns to gauge individual personality traits.

SUMMARY

In the process of your reading, you will have begun with looking at <u>both</u> hands together. Then you would have looked exclusively at the <u>left hand</u>, which represents development since childhood and moves on to the <u>right hand</u> which shows growth of attitudes and beliefs. You will notice differences. In practice, this means that your friend is changing and evolving as a person!

You are now in a position to summarise your findings.

A WORD ABOUT HONESTY

Honesty is important. Telling the truth is important. Do you know the truth? Remember that every human being is fallible and only God knows everything.

For this reason, be diplomatic and humble. Your words can heal or destroy. Choose them carefully. Both the hands are the lines upon them are in a constant state of change and like life itself, unpredictable. Give encouragement, support, and a positive approach. Never mention death or strong negative statements. Allow your friend to ask questions. Try to answer these honestly. Thank and bless them for the privilege of allowing you into their life.

TIME TO TEST YOURSELF

Here's your opportunity to examine your new found skills and learning. Let's imagine that Mary-Jo and Pedro Gonzalez are two of your friends and they have come to you for a reading!

TEST Write or tape-record your findings as if it were a real consultation. How do you perceive these people? What are their strengths and weaknesses? How could you help them? Next, refer to your notes to check your knowledge. Don't worry if you have made mistakes – we all do! What have you learnt?

MARY-JO'S HANDS

Hand Shape	She has a square palm and short fingers
Skin Ridge Patterns	She has a whorl print pattern on her index fingers. On her palms, a loop appears between the third and fourth fingers
Spacing/Setting	Her fingers are all wide spaced. Her little fingers are low set
Major Lines	Her Head line is low set. Her Heart line is high set
Minor lines	She possesses Medical Stigmata and Via Lascivia
Finger Phalanges	All Mary's lower base phalanges are well developed and full

ANSWERS:

Mary-Jo's **square hands** indicate she is practical, strong, reliable and methodical. **Whorl fingerprints** would point towards independence and self-reliance with the **Loop of Humour** showing her to be witty and fun loving.

The **wide spacing** of the fingers shows her to be extrovert with many interests. Her little finger shows insecurity and naïveté, but does indicate she gets on well with children.

As regards the **Major Lines**, the **Head Line** indicates someone who is imaginative and perceptive, although her heart rules her head. The **Heart Line** indicates she is demonstrative in affections.

With the **Minor Lines**, the presence of **Medial Stigmata** would indicate an ability in counselling, healing or therapies. The **Via Lascivia** would point towards metabolic sensitivity e.g. allergies, hypochondria or addictions to say coffee, alcohol or cigarettes.

The **Phalanges** show that Mary enjoys material comforts, e.g. food, drink, luxuries, possessions, sex, etc.

Mary-Jo is an Occupational Therapist specialising in paediatrics in a Senior Management position.

PEDRO GONZALEZ' HANDS

Hand Shape	He has a square palm and long, rounded fingers
Skin Ridge Patterns	On the middle fingers, he has the simple arch prints
Spacing/Setting	Pedro's fingers are wide spaced. His index finger is high low set
Major Lines	His Head line is long, in the high set position. His Heart line is in the low set position
Minor Lines	He has the Girdle of Venus well formed and the Ring of Solomon
	(Medium set) with the Teachers' Square
Finger Phalanges	All his lower base phalanges are well developed and full

ANSWERS:

Pedro Gonzalez' hand shape would indicate he is intellectual, discriminating and possessing good reasoning powers. **Simple Arch fingerprints** would point towards practical abilities at work, e.g. crafts, machinery or social skills.

The **wide spacing** of the fingers shows him to be extrovert with wide interests and the **Setting** of the index finger shows him to be assertive and confident possibly even domineering.

As regards the **Major Lines,** the **Head Line** indicates Pedro is rational, logical, equipped with excellent analytical skills or psychological insights. The **Heart Line** indicates he is undemonstrative in love, i.e. he mentalises his feelings.

With the **Minor Lines**, the presence of **Girdle of Venus** indicates underlying strong, powerful emotions, as well as dreams, fantasies and role-playing skills.

The **Ring of Solomon** shows he has intuitive gifts (psychological abilities) and the **Teachers' Square** would indicate an ability to teach.

Pedro is a Psychotherapist. He teaches remedial craft skills at a hospital.

JOHN HARRISON

BIOGRAPHY OF A PALMIST

Born in West London, John possessed the "intuitive gifts" of clairvoyance, clair-sentience, and visions since childhood. Being naturally creative, he wrote poetry from an early age, and later expanded into writing short stories and songs lyrics. Although not academically bright due to dyslexia, he studied English, Religion, Law, as well as Politics and chose to go into retail and sales management to begin his first career path.

However, John's primary interest was in Religion. In his teenage years, he studied Astrology and Palmistry and began practicing Yoga, Meditation, and Tai Chi Chan; because of his fascination for Taoism and Hinduism. This found fruition when he became the Chairman of the Theosophical Society [Alcott Lodge]; he was organising and attending lectures taught by the leading religious authorities of those days. He also lectured himself, having written his Thesis on Palmistry Counselling, the profession he was very fond of.

Not content with just being a student, having experienced "Samadhi", John began a lifelong Quest to discover the truth of being, and the Path to Self-Realisation and Spiritual Enlightenment. He learned that in all the major religions there were references to the Word of God [sound vibrations], and Knowledge of God [Light frequencies]. While this philosophy was intellectually appealing; the Mind never becomes enlightened.

So he began the search for a Perfect Master; one who could reveal by their Grace, the Truth of Being. Having participated in a whole succession of "spiritual paths," where teachers purported to take the aspirant on a journey to enlightenment, but failed to mention that they themselves were NOT enlightened, many illusions were experienced! However, fortunately in 2004, he finally found a true Path, with a Perfect Master and joined The Path of Light and Sound, where he hoped to complete his journey to Liberation during this life!

On the work front, regrettably after recession and austerity, John's family retail business reached its nemesis in 1988, when his parents Alan and Joyce retired. Unemployed for the first time in years, he took this opportunity to travel around the world, experiencing many diverse cultures, while revelling in their traditions and spiritual ceremonies. Upon return, he began to train as an Aromatherapist and Spiritual Healer, going on to become a psychotherapist, hypnotherapist, Seichem Tera Mai Healing Master, as well as studying Tantra and Chi Kung. With the experience gathered, he started the Smile Holistic Practice.

In 1989, he was involved in a serious car accident while travelling around India, but miraculously escaped virtually unscathed. Upon returning to England, John sought treatment at a local Mind, Body, and Soul Exhibition. It was a wonderful experience; that was when he found out that such Exhibitions occurred all over the country, where Tarot Readers, Clairvoyants, and Palmists could earn a living by giving Readings to an appreciative public.

In recent years, John has been published in leading magazines, as well as appeared on national T.V. and radio, given lectures on Palmistry Counselling in the U.S.A where his exemplary knowledge and experience dispelled many of the myths about Palmistry, and he was accorded great respect by their teachers who sent their students to purchase his home tuition palmistry counselling manuals, and get their readings!

Palmistry Counselling is the new career that he has established. It is a collaboration of the skills of Hand Analysis [Chirology], married to the Art of Hand Divination [Palmistry], which is rooted in the philosophy of Alchemy, Metaphysical Heurism and Ontology, and the psychological insights of the counsellor. Palmistry Counselling is a therapeutic discipline, aimed at empowering clients to attain their full potential in health, careers, and relationships.

In conclusion, Palmistry Counselling is a practical discipline that offers insights into our purpose in life. For those seeking answers to questions, a good grounding in metaphysics and philosophy is necessary. Then beyond palmistry, the path to Self-Realisation and Enlightenment can be found.

For private readings, party bookings, exhibition or corporate events, articles, lectures, T.V or Radio Appearances, or to learn Palmistry Counselling, contact John Harrison via his Website;-

www.john-harrison-palmistry.com

SMILE HOLISTIC PRACTICE

HOW TO CONTACT THE AUTHOR, TO OBTAIN A PAID FOR PALMISTRY READING.

Web-site www.john-harrison-palmistry.com

GENERAL PALMISTRY COUNSELLING CONSULTATION

This consultation will give you a general over-view of your life. The key areas that will be covered will be appertaining to health, careers and significant relationships in love. There will be specific guidance and counselling regarding Health Maintenance, and any recommended changes to a persons life-style necessary to improve health and vitality. The range of suitable occupations will be discussed and compatibility in love assessed.

INTERMEDIATE PALMISTRY COUNSELLING CONSULTATION

Covering the whole of your life, this has been a very popular consultation over the years! Because your health is probably the most important aspect of your life, we begin providing you with a useful insight into your strengths and weaknesses, in relation to the health of your body, mind and soul. Practical advice is given on how to maintain a healthy life-style, address any health issues, or face health challenges. Next in focusing upon your unique individual skills, we map out potential studies, or your career pathway. Finally, whilst you may know your own personality and character, what type of person would you be attracted to, in love. We have so many choices in modern life, but who will be your soul mate, on life's rich journey?

ADVANCED PALMISTRY COUNSELLING CONSULTATION

Over the years many clients have expressed their desire to have a consultation wherein they could ask questions regarding events in their lives. This consultation fulfils that ambition. From the timing of when to move house, to those who wish to give up paid work, to become self-employed, or to go back to work, having been a mother, there are many circumstances where advice is useful. Sometimes it is simply a question of having enough money to retire? And in love many people are still seeking their soul mate, that special person, to share life with.

On occasions, regrettably a person may have lost a loved one, and need counselling and guidance. In general most people realise that life can be subject to unexpected changes, and whilst at the time these can be undesirable, they can turn out for the best. There will generally be more advice at all stages of this consultation, and counselling with regards to career changes. Past and present activities will be discussed with potential paths into the future indicated.

COMPREHENSIVE PALMISTRY COUNSELLING CONSULTATION

This is an excellent consultation for those seeking in depth insight and genuine, honest counselling. Often it is difficult to make important decisions, or to see oneself as others may see us. Modern life is complex and sometimes we lack the skills or have insufficient self-awareness to realise our potential?

Therefore a detached objective but compassionate view is helpful. This reading focuses on our own unique psychology and philosophy towards life as well as taking into account our individual spiritual perspective. It is very much about attaining balance and homeostasis, and finding contentment.

Many people suffer from phobias, allergies, or have suffered from traumas such as grief, and have lost direction. Others are compulsive/obsessive or addictive types; who although they may be affluent, are deeply unhappy.

Fortunately, with my skills as an experienced multi-skilled professional therapist, often I can offer unique insights or suggest solutions to even some of life's most intractable health problems.

There are many lessons to learn in life, but are we learning them or simply becoming more bitter and perhaps reclusive.? This consultation addresses the bigger picture. Why have we come into this particular life, and what lessons do we need to learn? Where do we go from here? Forward into a transformative bright new future where we take control of our own destiny; or backwards into past traumas and re-occuring nightmares? The future is in your hands, so have the courage to change, and make this life meaningful!

HOW TO TAKE DIGITAL PHOTOS OF YOUR HANDS

Now Prepare your handprints as shown below and email or post them to me to process your order by visiting my web-site:- www.john-harrison-palmistry.com

METHOD ONE ----Send your hand digital photos by E-mail.

This is by far the quickest, easiest and less messy of the methods. You will ideally need someone to take the photos for you

1. Place your hands in front of a dark background ie not light coloured.
2. Take 2 photos, one of each hand and one set of each finger-print pattern (including thumbs) angled straight on ie not side views.

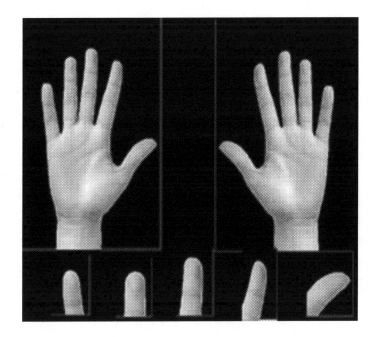

For more information kindly watch the video on my Web-site, to see how to send me your photos.

These can be e mailed from your Mobile Phone, or Computer to:- smile4u2024@yahoo.co.uk

Payments can be made via Credit/Debit Card or Pay Pal.

Meditation and Personal Development

To learn to relax, release stress, find peace, serenity, balance, and patience, or to go on the journey leading to self- realisation and spiritual enlightenment, visit my Website:-

www.meditation-4u2.com

www.smileholistictherapies.com

Palmistry Counselling by John Harrison, one of World's Experts on Palmistry.

Follow Me on Social Media at

https://www.facebook.com/people/John-Harrison/1784112544

https://twitter.com/palmistryjohn

SMILE HOLISTIC PRACTICE

PALMISTRY COUNSELLING

(guidance on health, careers, relationships, private readings,

party bookings, tuition and lectures)

MEDITATION TEACHER [guidance upon spiritual development]

(relax, feel peace, discover the real you!)

CHI KUNG

[stand, flow, store chi, re-energise]

MR JOHN HARRISON – MASTER PALMISTRY COUNSELLOR

Websites: http://john-harrison-palmistry.com

http://smileholistictherapies.com,

http://meditation-4u2.com

E Mail Consultations *Talks *Workshops*Corporate Events

*Private Consultations *Party Bookings

With thanks to contributors

Images by http://www.scottgaunt.co.uk

Compiled by Mike Davey at http://homebusinesszone.co.uk

Printed in the United States
By Bookmasters